On the Campaign Trail

~

J. Bradley

On the Campaign Trail
© 2020 J. Bradley
All rights reserved.

Edited by Joseph Demes
Designed by Joshua Bohnsack

Printed in the United States of America
Long Day Press LLC
Chicago, IL
www.LongDayPress.com
@LongDayPress

On the Campaign Trail

~

J. Bradley

Long Day Press

Chicago • Portland

Contents

**Campaign Stop:
Lakeland, FL**

Senator Minotaur steps back from the podium and cleaves it in twain. He brandishes the axe for everyone sitting in the front row to see. The camera zooms in on the axehead, giving the rest of the Lakeland Civic Center a clear view of some of the notches on the handle, the bloodstains.

Senator Minotaur just stands there, breathing softly, but firmly, his mouth kept closed, axe held steady (just like he practiced in the bathroom mirror last night).

You did well, Senator Minotaur's campaign manager says, careful to pat the Senator's shoulder with the one hand he has left.

Campaign Stop:
Parkland, FL

The attendees' jaws go slack after Senator Minotaur bends and then snaps an AR-15.

Does this mean you're actually for gun control? a man wearing a 'Make America Bleed Again' hat asks.

The Senator picks up one of the broken pieces of the rifle and begins stepping off the podium. It takes all of the Senator's Secret Service detail and his campaign staff to stop him from answering the man's question.

Barnes & Noble:
Orlando, FL

Senator Minotaur looks for the right book to read to the son he and his wife are planning to adopt.

Helps with your optics, his campaign manager had said.

When the Senator met his wife, they agreed children would be impossible. Their love was forgiven, even accepted by their faith, but their offspring would be targets. *Will our adopted child be a boy?* his wife asked. The campaign manager nodded. She'd followed up with: *Will he have blonde hair and blue eyes?*

The Senator shuddered at the suggestion: a son that was what their country's values were made of, who could only be more American if his skin were red, white, and blue, his smile sparklers in July.

Sea World:
Orlando, FL

Senator Minotaur stares at himself in the bathroom mirror in the only bathroom big enough to hold him at this aquatic theme park. His campaign manager made sure that the Senator would be alone while the Senator composed himself.

You can't keep avoiding our greatest resource, his campaign manager said on the way here. *It's a vital part of our economy.*

Every day after the Senator's first love fell from the sky, he'd swum until he couldn't see land and would always wake up on the beach. The last time, the ocean whispered, *You don't belong to me. Not yet.*

**Campaign Stop:
Orlando, FL**

The press pool asks Senator Minotaur why he won't campaign outside of Florida anymore. His campaign manager remembers the reporter in Montana who wandered off of a cliff, the reporter in Iowa whose stolen car doubled as his coffin, the reporter in Texas with a smile no stomach should make.

Curry Ford Road and Bumby Ave, November 2003:
Orlando, FL

Saying the alphabet backwards is like casting a spell, so Citizen Minotaur refuses the officer's request on religious grounds. The officer thinks about this for a moment and then points to the scuffed white line cleaving the road in twain.

Citizen Minotaur takes a deep breath, restrains his exhale so the officer can't smell what's left of happy hour. He pretends the road is the ocean and walks the line, one foot in front of the other. He then extends his arms and touches his nose at the same time with each step.

Press Conference:
Washington D.C.

Senator Minotaur thinks of the only boy he'd ever kissed, the one who wanted to fly and eventually did. The Senator remembers the sea salt on the boy's neck, the boy's hands on the small of the Senator's back after, a goodbye before the boy attempted his escape from their labyrinthian orphanage. The Senator had tried swimming out to where the boy fell but his arms quit a quarter of the way.

The Senator's position on marriage has always been that it's between a male and a female, his campaign manager says to a reporter.

The Senator struggles not to correct him.

Bedroom 3:00 AM:
Winter Park, FL

Senator Minotaur stands in front of the classroom naked as he does whenever the teacher calls on him to deliver his presentation on Greek mythology even though the Senator is proof that Greek mythology should be renamed something based in truth but mythology was invented by humans to explain away things that they refused to come up with an explanation for like lightning and winter and echoes and hepatitis and grief and death and the thing that calms him down is the possibility that there is a god that he can finally fistfight for making him the way he is.

About the Author

J. Bradley is the author of *Greetings from America: Letters from the Trade War* (Whiskey Tit Books, 2019). His flash fiction piece, "How to Burn a Bridge Job Aid" was selected for Best Small Fictions 2019. He lives at jbradleywrites.com.

LONG DAY PRESS

Dear Cowfolx,

Won't you buy our books? We haven't any finances to continue to produce books and your support would be appreciated.

Maybe you would like Kevin Sterne's *I've Done Worse*. It's a short story collection that George Saunders himself would be ashamed to be compared to.

No, you're right. You can't handle that. You're an abstract sorta folk. You're someone who could love Kenta Maniwa's *Someone Else's Toothbrush*.

No? You're right, you're always right. You're better than that. Well, how about Rebecca van Laer's poetry chapbook, *Don't Nod*?

Well, let me throw this out there: a hybrid chapbook of devotional Coldplay hymns? Where else can you find that besides with James Ardis's *A Head Full of Dreams*? Nowhere. No where.

I didn't think you were that fancy anyway. Well, I guess, you just have to stick with Chase Griffin's novel *What's On the Menu?* and that's how life works. We don't make the rules. Sorry and you're welcome.

Shameless/ful self-promotion.

CPSIA information can be obtained
at www.ICGtesting.com
Printed in the USA
LVHW041907090220
646370LV00002B/7

9 781950 987047